TAKE CARE!

POISONOUS AUSTRALIAN ANIMALS

DR STRUAN SUTHERLAND, M.D.
and **SUSIE KENNEWELL, B.A.**

HYLAND HOUSE

ALSO BY DR STRUAN SUTHERLAND

Dangerous Australian Animals

Hydroponics for Everyone

A Venomous Life

ACKNOWLEDGEMENTS

The cartoons were kindly drawn by Leonie Stott and the photographs provided by expert friends. Special thanks is due to Dr Jeanette Covacevich, Keith Gillett, Graeme Gow, Dr Mike Gray, Dr Robert Hartwick, Peter Mirtschin, Prof. John Pearn, Dr Robert Raven, Prof. Mike Taylor, John and Robyn Weigel and Prof. John Williamson. Dr James Tibballs and the Australian Resuscitation Council advised on first aid. Finally the ongoing assistance of Dr Ken Winkel, Dr Gabrielle Hawdon and Vanessa Tresidder, all of the Australian Venom Research Unit, is greatly appreciated.

First edition published in 1983
Second edition published in 1992
This third revised and enlarged edition published in 1999 by
Hyland House Publishing Pty Ltd (www.hylandhouse.com.au)
Reprinted 2005 and 2012

National Library of Australia
cataloguing-in-publication data:
    Sutherland, Struan K. (Struan Keith), 1936-.
    Take care!: poisonous Australian animals.
    3rd ed.
    ISBN 1 86447 068 2.
    1. Poisonous animals - Australia - Juvenile literature. I. Kennewell,
    Susie. II. Title
591.650994

Design and layout by Captured Concepts, Melbourne
Cartoons by Leonie Stott
Printed in China by Everbest

Introduction

Holidays in the country or by the sea are great fun—much better than being at school. Who wants to have a fabulous holiday messed up by an angry snake or ruined by jellyfish stings? No one! The purpose of this book is to say something about our most important poisonous creatures—some of which are the most dangerous in the world—and explain how not to be hurt by them. None of these creatures are particularly keen to bite or sting people, but sadly this often happens, and so the modern types of first aid are explained.

No sensible person goes off camping for a few days without the right clothes, good equipment and plenty of tucker. All campers should spare a few moments to learn how to avoid poisonous bites and stings. They can then settle down to enjoy the wonders of nature in the countryside rather than end up reading about them in a hospital bed.

DEDICATION

To all children who have died of snake bites —
especially Maree V. aged 3 years.

Contents

Why some animals have a poisonous bite or sting

All animals need food and the venomous ones like fresh food. They use their poison to kill their prey quickly with as little trouble as possible. Why get into a fight when you can win with a secret weapon?

Snakes and spiders have two hollow teeth (fangs) which can put poison (venom) into the creatures they bite. The venom is made in two sacs like very small plastic bags and it is squeezed out as the fangs go into the victim, often an insect or mouse. The venom kills the victim quickly so that the snake or spider can eat its dinner in peace and quiet.

Some animals, like jellyfish, have millions of tiny stinging spikes which are fired into prawns or fish. They die in seconds.

If people are poisoned by dangerous snakes or spiders the venom may slowly damage the nerves of their bodies so that they may become weaker and weaker. They may even die some hours later if they are not treated by a doctor.

The good news is that all hospitals have special medicines (antivenoms) which can quickly stop the venom working. Before antivenoms were made, many children and adults died from bites and stings. Nowadays they almost always get better and go home the next day with rather an exciting story to tell their mates!

SPECIAL NOTE FOR PARENTS!

Never let children collect snakes. If young children say they have had contact with a snake, please believe them. Remember that a young child may sometimes describe the snake as a stick, a rope, or just a 'bitey'. One little girl described the snake that bit her as a 'monster'!

How to avoid bites and stings

Snake bite

* Leave snakes alone.
* Wear shoes, socks and jeans in 'snake country'. Do not wear sandals or thongs.
* Never put your hands into hollow logs or thick grass without looking first.
* Turn your shoes upside down and shake them before putting them on.
* When in the bush, check your sleeping bag, towel and clothes before using them.
* Always use a torch around camps and farm-houses at night. Remember most snakes are active on summer nights.
* Make sure barns and sheds are kept free of mice and rats that may attract snakes, and help keep the grass well cut, particularly in play-grounds and other places you go to.

Spider bite

Don't touch spiders! 99.9 per cent of them have fangs and can poison you, even though most are not likely to make you sick. Take special care in places like the backs of sheds, or outside toilets, or when playing near old rubbish, wood heaps, etc.

Dangerous sea creatures

Don't swim in the sea by yourself and never go into the sea in the tropics when Box Jellyfish are about. Always wear runners if exploring tropical reefs. Diving boots are ideal for this purpose. Never pick up octopuses or any other sea creatures without asking if they are poisonous. Wear gloves when touching fish.

First aid

Snake bite

Even though some snakes are not dangerous it is best to treat all snake bites as if they were dangerous and give the victim first aid. A snake usually bites near the ankle or the hand so it is easy to use first aid. Remember, never make cuts over the snake bite or put a tight bandage around the top of the leg or arm, but use the correct method of first aid described below. Don't wash the bitten area because hospitals do a special test on the fang marks. This lets the doctor know what type of snake has made the bite.

First aid for snake bite: the 'Pressure-immobilisation method'

Look at the pictures on pages 9 and 10.

1 Put a broad, firm bandage around the limb and on the bitten area. Crepe bandages are best, but any flexible material will do; for example, you can tear up clothing or old towels into strips. Pantyhose is also suitable.

2 The bandage should be as tight as you would bind a sprained ankle.

3 Bandage as much of the limb as possible.

4 Keep the limb as still as possible. Bind some type of splint to the limb—a piece of timber, a spade, or anything that doesn't bend.

5 Take the victim to a doctor or hospital as quickly as possible. Try to bring a car to the victim. If that's impossible see if you can make a stretcher and carry him or her to the car. Remember, if possible the victim should be carried rather than allowed to walk, regardless of where the bite has occurred.

6 Leave the bandages and splint on until medical care is reached. It's a good idea to practise this kind of first aid sometimes, especially if you live in the country or will be going into the bush for a holiday.

PRESSURE-IMMOBILISATION TYPE OF FIRST AID FOR BITES ON THE LEG

1 Starting from the toes put a broad firm bandage round the bitten area. Don't take off any clothes like jeans but cut the seams if they can't be pushed out of the way, and keep the leg as still as possible while you are bandaging.

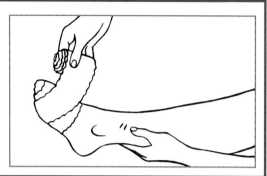

2 Make the bandage as tight as for a sprained ankle.

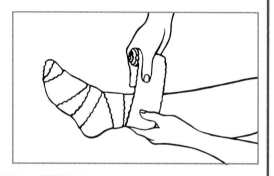

3 Bandage as much of the leg as possible, especially the toes.

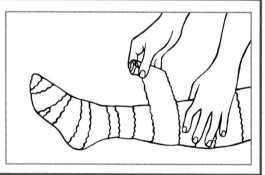

4 Put a splint beside the bandage and bind that to the leg to help keep the leg still.

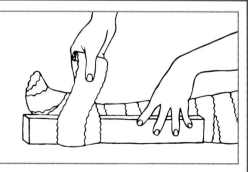

PRESSURE-IMMOBILISATION TYPE OF FIRST AID FOR BITES TO HAND OR ARM

1 Put a broad, firm bandage round the bitten area up to the elbow. Start from the fingers and bandage as much of the arm as possible. Make sure the victim can still bend the elbow.

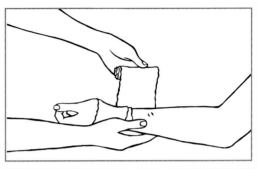

2 Put a splint under the arm and bind it to the arm.

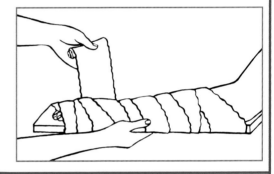

3 Put the arm in a sling.

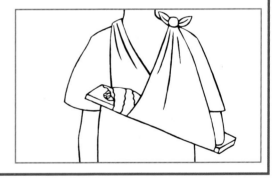

The bandages and splint should be quite comfortable so that they can be left on for several hours. They should not be taken off until the victim has reached a doctor or hospital. The doctor will decide when to remove the bandages.

Spider bite

The Pressure-immobilisation type of first aid is used also for Funnel-web spider bites and Mouse spider bites. Red-back spider bites don't need any special first aid because their venom works very slowly. Just take the victim (and spider in a jar) to hospital as soon as possible. If the Red-back spider bite is painful, put a plastic bag filled with a little ice and water on the painful area. You could also use a packet of frozen peas wrapped in a towel.

   No special first aid is required for bites by other spiders, such as the White-tailed spider, the Black House or Window spider and Huntsman spiders. Usually very little effect is produced by their bites. If the bite is painful, put a plastic bag filled with a little ice and water over the painful area.

Australian Paralysis tick

The tick should be carefully removed as soon as possible (see page 47). If the victim is feeling ill and the bite is on the arm or leg, use the Pressure-immobilisation type of first aid, if possible, to slow the movement of any poison that has been squeezed out of the tick during its removal.

Bee stings

Scrape or pull the sting and venom sac off the stung area as quickly as possible and put a plastic bag filled with a little ice and water on the stung area.

European and English wasps, and Jumper, Bull and Blue ants

Put a plastic bag filled with a little ice and water over the stung area.

CARDIOPULMONARY RESUSCITATION (CPR) IN BASIC LIFE SUPPORT

1 Send for help. Place the victim flat on the back on a hard surface. Lift up the jaw. Look, listen and feel for breathing.
* Look at the chest.
* Listen for breathing sounds.
* Feel for breath.

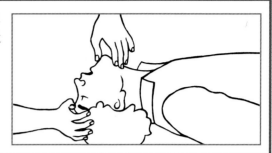

2 If the victim is not breathing, begin expired air resuscitation (mouth to mouth or nose breathing)—5 slow breaths to make the chest rise and fall, then ...

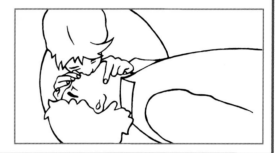

3 Check the pulse in the neck. If the pulse is absent, begin external cardiac compression. Depress the lower half of the sternum (breast bone) one-third the depth of the chest at a rate of 100/minute (5 times in 3 seconds).

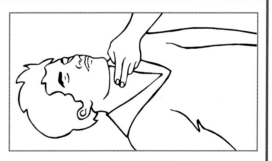

4 Combine external cardiac compression and expired air resuscitation in a ratio of 5:1 (5 compressions then 1 breath in 5 seconds) for babies and children, but in a ratio of 15:2 for adults (15 compressions then 2 breaths in 15 seconds) whether there are 1 or 2 rescuers. Continue uninterrupted until trained assistance arrives.

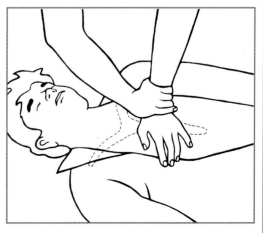

Severe reactions to Bee, European and English wasp and Jumper and Bull ant stings

If you know that the person who has been stung is sensitive to these stings and may suffer a severe reaction, apply the Pressure-immobilisation type of first aid to the stung area. Assist the victim's breathing using CPR if necessary (see opposite) and take the victim to a doctor or hospital as soon as possible.

Platypus sting

Do not apply the Pressure-immobilisation type of first aid. Ice and water may give some relief from pain, but most patients need an injection of painkillers by a doctor.

Blue-Ringed octopus and Conus shells

Use the Pressure-immobilisation method.

CPR or some other type of help with breathing may be needed also. The pictures on the opposite page tell you how to do this.

Box jellyfish or 'Sea wasp'

As soon as possible pour kitchen vinegar over the tentacles to kill them. Never use methylated spirits or alcohol.

Irukandji

Apply kitchen vinegar to the stung area. All people stung by Irukandji should be seen by a doctor.

Blue Bottle or Portuguese Man-of-War

Stings from this creature are treated by washing any tentacles off with water (not vinegar) and then putting a plastic bag filled with a little ice and water over the stung area.

Stingrays

Put a plastic bag filled with a little ice and water over the stung area. If bleeding occurs, apply firm pressure over the area. All Stingray stings should be seen by a doctor.

Stonefish and other stinging fish

Try bathing the sting in warm water. Antivenom and special drugs will be needed for bad Stonefish stings. Stings from other fish are very painful, but usually the pain does not last long.

Crown of Thorns starfish and Black Sea Urchin

Carefully pull out any spines, bathe in warm water or apply ice and water to ease the pain and go to a doctor or hospital.

Cane Toads

Wash exposed area very well. If some poison has been swallowed see page 79.

Snakes

Snakes are reptiles. They are cold-blooded animals and are usually more active after they have been warmed up by the sun. They shed their skin regularly and go into hiding while this is happening. Since a snake has no eyelids it gives a steady, unblinking look which frightens many people. Its eyesight and sense of smell is quite good but it is completely deaf. It picks up vibrations from the ground through its body so it's a good idea, if snakes are about, for you to stomp along (in boots) as loudly as possible. If the snake feels you are coming, it will slither away long before you get there.

Some funny stories are told about snakes which are not true. Snakes don't swallow their young to protect them. If they do eat another snake it's for their dinner! Snakes will die any time, not just at sunset. A saucer of milk will not attract a snake, nor will music. Snakes are just snakes and are not magical except in some stories. Like most animals, they only want to be left alone to live their lives in peace, and usually bite people only when they are frightened. Some snakes lay eggs and others produce their babies alive.

There are more than 100 types of snakes in Australia and at least 18 are dangerous to people. Some of the most important ones are described in this book.

Tasmanian Tiger snake sunning itself

1 Tiger Snakes

Tiger snakes usually have yellowish stripes like a tiger and when they're annoyed they can be as dangerous as real tigers!

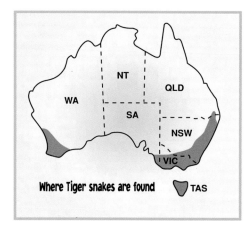

Where Tiger snakes are found

There are also black Tiger snakes, which live in the south-west of Western Australia, the Flinders Ranges in South Australia,Tasmania and the Bass Strait Islands. They don't have yellow stripes, but they're just as dangerous so look out for them too!

Tiger snakes grow to about 1 metre in length. They don't lay eggs. Even the newborn baby snakes can bite and should never be touched!

They are often found near rivers and dams and they love eating frogs. They also like mice and on hot summer evenings will hunt them round farms and outer suburban houses. They will even come into kitchens and bedrooms!

AN ANGRY TIGER SNAKE WOULD SCARE A REAL TIGER!

Snake bites are often caused by Tiger snakes so be very careful on summer evenings when they are out hunting.

FIRST AID

For Tiger snake bites— Pressure-immobilisation method, see pages 8-10.

Photo: John Weigel

2 Brown Snakes

Where Brown snakes are found

There are a number of types of Brown snakes and they are all very dangerous. The most important is the Eastern or Common Brown snake. Its colour varies from light brown to very dark brown and it is slender and very fast moving. It may grow as long as 2.4 metres.

Brown snakes prefer dry places and often come around farms looking for mice and rats, which they enjoy eating. Unlike the Tiger snakes, the Brown snakes lay eggs, but like them they are deadly. Their venom is the second most poisonous in Australia. When a Brown snake is angry it may wind itself up into an 'S' shape and so people are often bitten on the knee or higher.

Apart from catching rats, the only good thing about this snake is that it is the only very dangerous Australian snake that usually goes to sleep when the sun sets. Unfortunately, sometimes it goes to sleep in a camper's sleeping bag! So don't forget to shake your bag out before tucking yourself up for the night.

FIRST AID

For Brown snake bites—
Pressure-immobilisation
method, see pages 8-10.

3 Red-bellied Black Snake

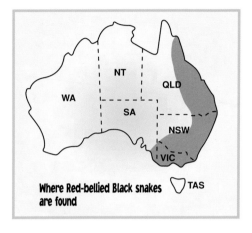

Where Red-bellied Black snakes are found

When the white settlers arrived in eastern Australia, they found the bush absolutely teeming with these snakes. Needless to say, they were scared stiff and tried to kill off as many as they could. In fact one wealthy settler, knowing that there were no wild snakes in Ireland, actually brought out a shipload of Irish soil to put around his house in the hope that it would keep the snakes away. (It didn't work!)

It may grow to 2.5 metres and its red sides and tummy make it easy to see. The babies are born alive, not in eggs.

It has a fairly gentle nature and generally will only bite if it is really annoyed.

It loves swimming and is very fond of eating other snakes, even other Red-bellied Black snakes. It is not very often seen in zoos as it tends quietly to eat up all the other snakes when no-one is watching!

FIRST AID

For Red-bellied Black snake bites— Pressure-immobilisation method, see pages 8-10.

Photo: Peter Mirtschin

4 Copperhead Snake

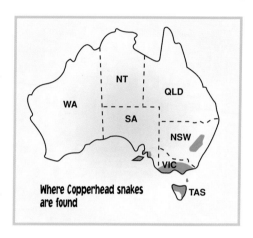

Where Copperhead snakes are found

Although Copperheads are very poisonous, they don't often bite people unless they have been really frightened. For instance, one man got very sick when he jumped off his tractor, and landed on a sleeping Copperhead, which woke in a fright and bit him.

Apart from being mild-mannered, Copperheads have a few other special features. They are the only dangerous Australian snake that really loves cold weather. They like to be out and about on mountains. If it's really freezing then they might go and have a snooze in an animal burrow. But if they find a small animal in the burrow they'll have dinner first, then a snooze! When the sun comes out and the snows are melting the Copperhead will be the first creature out sunbaking. So skiers watch out!

A Copperhead that has just shed its skin can look absolutely beautiful in the sunlight. This snake's colours vary from dark brown to a polished light copper. Their average length is 1.2 metres and they love

COPPERHEAD SNAKES CAN GOBBLE THEIR BABIES, IF FOOD IS SCARCE.

Photo: Peter Mirtschin

swimming. If there are plenty of frogs about, the low-land variety of Copperhead may gather for a big party around the swamps.

Copperheads may have as many as twenty babies a year, and they are all born as little snakes rather than hatching from eggs. These little snakes have to keep their wits about them because if food is scarce their parents are apt to gobble them up!

FIRST AID

For Copperhead snake bites—
Pressure-immobilisation method, see pages 8-10.

Death Adder

This is a very dangerous snake that looks quite different from other Australian snakes. Its body can be 1 metre long, is thick and ends in a funny little spiky tail. This snake does not lay eggs.

Where Death Adders are found

The worst thing about this snake is that it likes to come out at night and lie half-buried in leaves on bush tracks. It sneakily wiggles its little tail and then kills any mouse or rat that wanders up to see what's going on. Other snakes usually move away if they know a human is walking towards them, but not the Death Adder! It stays perfectly still and bites very quickly if it is touched.

Its fangs are long and the venom is very strong. Some people call these snakes 'Deaf Adders' since they don't get out of the way when someone walks towards them. However, like all snakes, they do not have proper ears but pick up the vibrations from the ground as the human tramps along.

Use a torch at night and you are much less likely to be bitten by a Death Adder.

FIRST AID

For Death Adder bites—
Pressure-immobilisation
method, see pages 8-10.

6 Taipan

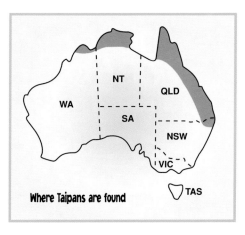

Where Taipans are found

This is the longest highly venomous snake in Australia and may reach 3.35 metres in length. The young hatch out of eggs. A Taipan is very shy and people often don't know that they have been near one. This is just as well because, if cornered, it can be most vicious. Often the Taipan bites again and again—so quickly that it is just a blur. Its fangs are the longest of any Australian snake (the record is 13 millimetres).

Until an antivenom was made, most people bitten by Taipans died because of the strength and amount of venom it injects. One little boy of four was attacked by a Taipan and died a few minutes later. It is most unusual for people to die so quickly but he had a great many bites.

Taipans often hunt near farm buildings or on garbage tips. They feed on rats and mice and will sometimes catch birds. When they are 'milked' of their venom in the laboratory the average amount of venom taken from each snake is enough to kill 12,000 guinea pigs! Thank heavens Taipans are usually frightened by people and race off in the opposite direction!

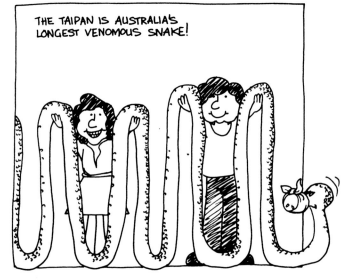

THE TAIPAN IS AUSTRALIA'S LONGEST VENOMOUS SNAKE!

Photo: Vern Draffin

FIRST AID

For Taipan bites—
Pressure-immobilisation
method, see pages 8-10.

7 Mulga Snake

This is Australia's heaviest dangerous snake. It is sometimes called the 'King Brown snake', although it is not related to the Brown snakes described in this book. It grows to over 3 metres in length and produces more venom than any other Australian snake. In fact it is the world champion venom producer.

Although the venom is not quite as strong as that of the other common poisonous snakes, a bite by this snake may still be very serious. It often makes a few big bruises around the bites as its big heavy head strikes against the person. The bites are usually painful and cause a lot of swelling.

The Mulga snake eats many rats, mice, lizards and birds as well as other snakes. Rabbit burrows make a fine home for the snake and its eggs. Mulga snakes taste good and are a favourite food of Aborigines and bushmen, although shopping for this particular dinner has often proved more dangerous than a visit to the super-market!

THE MULGA SNAKE IS THE HEAVIEST VENOMOUS SNAKE!

WEIGHT WATCHERS MEETING

FIRST AID

For Mulga snake bites— Pressure-immobilisation method, see pages 8-10.

8 Small-scaled Snake

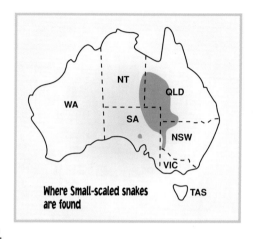

Where Small-scaled snakes are found

This snake, which is also called the 'Fierce snake', caused a lot of excitement amongst scientists when it was found alive in Western Queensland in 1976. This was the first time it had been seen for about 100 years! Since then, many more have been found and the venom has been tested in the laboratory.

To everyone's surprise, the Small-scaled snake has the **most poisonous snake venom in the world**. Fortunately, there have been very few records of people being bitten by this snake, but now that it is being kept in zoos and collections, bites have become more common!

IF YOU SEE A SNAKE, ALWAYS LEAVE IT ALONE.

ZZZZZZ

The Small-scaled snake is closely related to the Taipan and some people call it the 'Western Taipan'. Its colour is darker than the Taipan and the longest one found so far measured 1.93 metres. Like the Taipan it lays eggs, but is far better tempered and would probably have to be hit with a stick before it became a 'fierce snake'! Usually it lives in deep cracks in the ground where it feeds on rats. The amount of venom it can produce is enough to kill 250,000 mice—so it's best left alone!

FIRST AID

For Small-scaled snake bites—
Pressure-immobilisation method, see pages 8-10.

9 Sea Snakes

Where Sea snakes are found

At least 26 types of Sea snake swim about in the tropical waters of Australia. Sometimes one will be found down south. Many are quite poisonous but they don't often bite people. The first aid for a sea snake bite is the same as for land snakes but the doctor may have to give the victim a Sea snake antivenom. If this is not handy, then Tiger snake antivenom can be used.

Sea snakes are easily identified because they have a paddle-shaped tail. Most spend all their lives at sea. Sometimes, they meet together in huge crowds called *slicks* drifting along on the surface of the sea. They can take a huge breath and then dive quickly deep under the sea to catch fish or prawns. They have a big lung that goes almost the whole length of their bodies. For some snakes this allows them to stay under the water for several hours and to dive as deep as 100 metres.

The babies of most Sea snakes are born at sea, although one type wriggles ashore and

THAT THIN LOG IN THE SEA MIGHT SUDDENLY COME TO LIFE!

lays eggs. Sea snakes shed their skin at least once a month so that their skin is always free from any slime which would slow them down.

Prawn fishermen know to watch out for Sea snakes, especially if they catch a group of them in a net at night. The crew quickly run to the other end of the boat—and one cannot blame them!

Sometimes eels are mistaken for Sea snakes and give people a fright. Eels are easy to recognise. They have no nostrils or scales, but they do have gills and fins as well as a good set of sharp (non-poisonous) teeth. They are fish, but Sea snakes are reptiles like the land snakes.

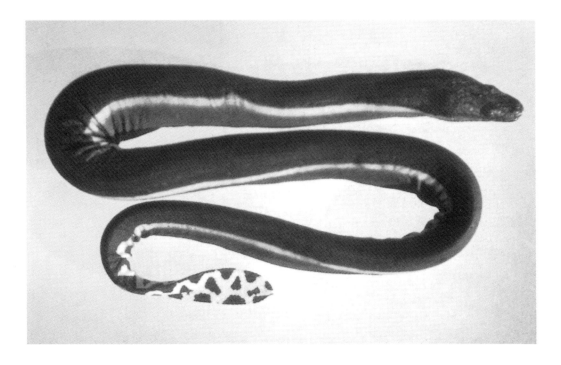

FIRST AID

For Sea snake bites—
Pressure-immobilisation
method, see pages 8-10.

10 Red-back Spider

Although it seems a good joke when this spider bites someone on the bottom while they are sitting on a toilet seat, the owner of the bottom is never amused!

Every year hundreds of Australians need Red-back spider antivenom—and most Red-back spider bites would not happen if people were more careful.

Where Red-back spiders are found

The Red-back is found in most gardens, in old sheds and other quiet, dark places, as well as out in the bush. Only the female's bite makes people ill and the bright red or orange stripe on her behind is one of nature's clearest warnings of danger.

LOOK BEFORE YOU SIT—ESPECIALLY ON COUNTRY TOILET SEATS!

YIKES

Usually she hides away in a corner of her untidy web, which she builds in some dark cool place, and only pops out when some insect or beetle has got stuck to the web. When she is guarding her egg sacs (and these may contain as many as 2,000 babies), she is more likely to bite any one who disturbs the web.

Generally the Red-back only bites human skin if it is pushed close to her, as when the owner comes to put on a pair of old jeans or gloves in which

(female pictured)

she made her home. People often get bitten when the spider is picked up with rubbish.

The Red-back's tiny bite hardly hurts at first but soon becomes very painful. After some hours the bitten person may have pain in other parts of the body and be sweating heavily. The victims do not get very sick for many hours and they all get better very quickly when given antivenom.

FIRST AID

For Red-back spider bites—
- Seek medical care.
- Do not panic! The venom works very slowly.
- If painful, place a bag of iced water on the bite.

11 Funnel-web Spiders

Australia could do without these spiders! The most important one is the Sydney Funnel-web spider, which is only found in an area covering 160 kilometres from the centre of Sydney. It really is the most dangerous spider in the world since its bites are known to have killed 3 children in less than 2 hours after they were bitten.

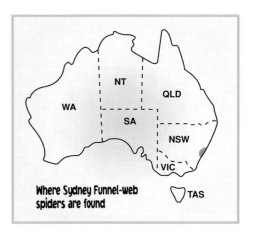

Where Sydney Funnel-web spiders are found

It is a very strange spider. The male Funnel-web kills people, while with other spiders the female is the most deadly. Its venom hardly makes dogs or cats sick at all, but if people are badly poisoned all their muscles may twitch, they sweat heavily, their heart beats terribly fast and then they become unconscious. Fortunately, most bitten people don't get much poison because usually the venom falls off the tips of the spider's big fangs just before the bite.

Funnel-web spiders like cool, damp places to live in, but when the male is grown up he becomes a wanderer. He likes to roam into houses, especial-

THE WORLD'S NASTIEST AND MOST DANGEROUS SPIDER

ly if heavy rain has made the outside too wet for walking about. He is very bad tempered and stands up high with his fangs ready to bite if anyone comes near him. Great care must be taken, especially at night, so that you don't walk on him or accidentally pick him up. Turn on the light or use

(male pictured)

a torch and wear slippers or shoes. Check for spiders before you pick up clothes or put them on.

The first aid for Funnel-web spider bite—which may save your life—is the same as for snake bite. Fortunately, an antivenom is available in hospitals which reduces the danger from this horrible spider.

FIRST AID

For Funnel-web spider bites—
Pressure-immobilisation method, see pages 8-10.

12 White-tailed Spider

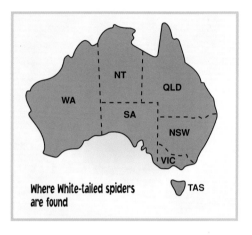

Where White-tailed spiders are found

This small spider is found at some time of the year in practically every house in Australia. It has a dark brown body, which is sausage-shaped. Usually it has a small white spot on the tip of its tail. Being a hunting spider, it does not spin a web, but quietly prowls around looking for some sleepy insect to grab. Other spiders make up a large part of its diet.

Quite often the White-tailed spider decides to have a rest in bedclothes or clothing that have been left on the floor. Bathroom towels are another favourite place. When the bed is made up, the White-tailed spider may find itself tucked in, deep amongst the sheets, wondering how on earth to get out. Later on when a sleepy human gets into the bed and starts to squash the spider it may give a small bite. The bite is usually fairly painless. In most cases it causes no damage, but sometimes the bitten area becomes very painful some hours later. A few people develop a nasty ulcer.

It is very important always to shake bedclothes, towels and clothes that have been left lying around for some time.

FIRST AID

For White-tailed spider bites—
See page 11.

CHECK YOUR BED
FOR A MANY LEGGED
AND MULTI-EYED VISITOR

13 Black House or Window Spider

This spider is found in most houses. It makes an untidy funnel-shaped web in the corner of windows and in crevices. The web itself looks a bit like lace. The Black House spider is about as black as a spider can be, and generally hides during the day. At night it can usually be

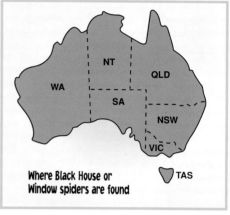

Where Black House or Window spiders are found

Photo: Dr Robert Raven

DON'T POKE YOUR FINGER IN THIS VERY BLACK SPIDER'S WEB!

seen pottering around repairing its web or wrapping up freshly caught prey.

A bite from this spider can be very painful and may develop into an ulcer. Some people have felt quite sick for a few hours after the bite and they may do a great deal of vomiting.

Nobody has been known to have died from this spider's bite, but it should be treated very carefully. Very large specimens are sometimes found in the bush. Be very careful when collecting firewood, and roll the logs over and inspect them closely before you pick them up.

FIRST AID

For Black House or Window spider bites— See page 11.

14 Huntsman Spiders

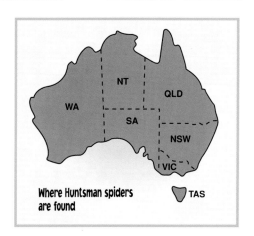

These spiders grow to be great big fellows and are quite common in houses throughout Australia in summer. Although they give people terrible frights, it is believed that most of them are harmless. They do have quite big fangs, but their venom is very weak and they only bite if they are being really roughly treated.

Where Huntsman spiders are found

We have put them in this book because lots of people are scared stiff of them. They call them 'Tarantulas', which they are not. Tarantulas are not found in Australia and, believe it or not, Tarantulas are thought to be quite harmless anyway!

Huntsman spiders do a very good job crawling across walls and ceilings, wiping out mosquitoes and other annoying creatures. The good thing about spiders is that they don't damage the environment or affect the ozone layer like some insect sprays.

We like to leave the Huntsman spiders roaming around our houses until they start getting quite large. Then they can be swept out of the house with a straw broom. It is best to be wide awake when doing this, as the spiders can duck and weave like a good footballer.

Huntsman spiders occasionally hide behind the sunshade in a car. When the driver lowers the sunshade, the spider drops onto his or her lap. Lots of things can happen in the next few seconds!

FIRST AID

For Huntsman spider bites—
See page 11.

Photo: Vern Draffin

15 The Mouse Spider

Where Mouse spiders are found

With its bright red head and fang bases, the male Mouse spider is very easy to identify. Mouse spiders are found everywhere in Australia, except Tasmania, and both male and female are dangerous. There are a number of types of Mouse spiders and unlike most spiders the males like to wander around in broad daylight. Some people have been terribly frightened sunbaking on a lawn and finding a large red-headed Mouse spider marching towards them.

Most Mouse spiders have very large fangs which open wide and cross over like pincers. When they rear back, venom can often be seen dripping

THE MOUSE SPIDER MAKES CUTE LITTLE SIDE TUNNELS WITH SILK AND EARTH DOORS FOR ITS BABIES.

HOME SWEET HOME

Photo: Susie Kennewell

from the tips of the fangs. The size of these squat, heavily built spiders varies considerably but usually they can comfortably cover a 20 cent coin.

The female digs a deep tunnel, which she lines with silk. She makes a little side tunnel for her babies and constructs cute little doors of silk and earth for both the nursery and the main entrance.

The venom works something like the Sydney Funnel-web spider venom. Fortunately bites are very rare and the Sydney Funnel-web spider antivenom has been useful treating some of the worst cases.

Why is it called a Mouse spider?

Perhaps because of the size of its tunnels and how it scuttles back into its tunnel.

FIRST AID

For Mouse spider bites— Pressure-immobilisation method, see pages 8-10.

16 Australian Paralysis Tick

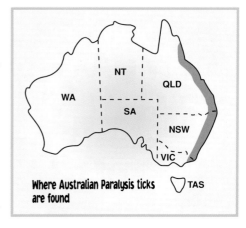

Where Australian Paralysis ticks are found

Sometimes these are called the Scrub or Bush tick.

A family picnic in 'tick country' may never be forgotten. Like female mosquitoes, ticks feed on the blood of animals through a little hole in their skin. They like hot meals and so feed only on warm blooded animals like people, dogs and cats. As the tiny tick quietly sucks up its dinner from your body, its saliva escapes into the skin. The saliva is poisonous and can weaken the nerves of its victim. It is the most dangerous tick in the world and at least 17 children have died from paralysis caused by its saliva in New South Wales alone since 1904.

The tick goes through three stages during its life and at each stage it must feed on blood. The last stage is the important one. The tiny nymph tick climbs to the tops of bushes hoping to be brushed onto a passing animal. Once on the animal the nymph, which is the size of a pin's head, buries its mouth parts into the skin. Over the next 3 or 4 days it fills itself with blood and may become as large as a child's finger nail. Then it usually falls off and lays its eggs but it may stay on the skin and, after a time, it will cause paralysis. The longer it stays, the more poisonous its saliva becomes.

Only the female tick feeds on animals; the male actually makes a hole on the female's back and drinks her blood. She doesn't seem to mind and even lets him mate at the same time!

After you have been in 'tick country' you should look for ticks on your body over the next few days. Get someone else to look into places you can't see like the top of your head or your ears.

Ticks should be removed by carefully levering them out. Curved scissors make a good tool and should be carried in the first aid kit if you are going to camp in bush where there are ticks. A doctor should be seen if you feel tired or weak. People sometimes lose their appetites, can't read easily or their muscles may feel stiff and clumsy if they are getting tick paralysis. Sometimes you never find the tick and you still fall ill. An antitoxin has been made and all patients who are treated in time now get better.

Look for ticks on your dog, too, especially in places like the ears. If he loses his appetite and looks ill or becomes clumsy when he is getting up and walking, take him to the vet and tell the vet he has been in 'tick country'.

FIRST AID

For Ticks—
- Look for ticks and remove them.
- Remember you can become ill even after you have removed the tick and for as long as 8 days after you have left 'tick country', so, if you feel ill, see a doctor and tell him or her you have been in 'tick country'.

17 The Honey Bee

Australia has some native bees, but the most important bee from every point of view is the Common or European Honey bee. These always seem busy; they spend most of their waking hours collecting nectar from flowers and bringing it back to the hive. If you disturb them, they can sting you with a very fine sting

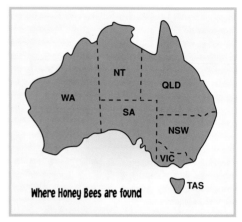

Where Honey Bees are found

that is pushed out from the end of their bodies. The sting has little barbs on it, and so once it is pushed into your skin, the bee cannot remove it. When the bee flies away, it leaves the sting and poison gland behind. This hurts the bee so much that it soon dies.

The poison that is injected down the sting causes an immediate sharp pain. If you don't get rid of the poison sac it will go on pumping poison down the sting and so the sting and poison sac should be removed as soon as possible by scraping them off with a finger nail or just quickly pulling them off.

Some people become very sensitive to bee venom. After a sting they may get a rash over their bodies or become very short of breath. Sometimes they even die.

BE KIND TO LITTLE BEES OR YOU'LL BEE SORRY!

OUCH

Fortunately, this allergy usually develops gradually and doctors have time to treat it before it gets too severe.

Never drink directly from a can of soft drink outside. Bees and wasps (see pages 50–1) can fly inside the can when you are not looking and, if you accidentally swallow a bee or a wasp, it may sting the back of your throat and you may choke to death. ALWAYS use a straw or pour the can into a glass.

Bees love the clover growing on lawns and you may get stung if you play barefooted in summer. Ask your mum or dad to spray the lawn to get rid of clover. Clover sprays are quite safe—but not for the clover!

FIRST AID

For Bee stings—
See pages 11–13.

18 European and English Wasps

Where European wasps are found

NT
QLD
WA
SA
NSW
VIC
TAS

Over the last few years, these wasps have been quietly spreading across the eastern parts of Australia and they are going to be an even bigger menace in the future. The map shows the area they covered in 1999. In Europe, many of the nests are destroyed by the cold winters, but in most parts of Australia they comfortably survive winter and get bigger and bigger each year. In Europe, the nests are often about the size of a football and perhaps contain 6,000 wasps. In Australia, some nests have been found more than 3 metres long and containing millions of wasps. The nests are usually at ground level and it is very dangerous to go near them, especially during the day. If you accidentally disturb a wasps' nest, many may attack you and the only thing to do is to run away as soon as possible. Most local councils will give you advice or arrange for the destruction of the nest.

The wasps are easy to spot because of their very bright yellow and dark brown colours. They do not appear to be frightened of anything, and will often zoom in on family barbecues in a most unpleasant way. Just like

WASPS CAN REALLY GET UP YOUR NOSE!

An English wasp (Photo: Vern Draffin)

bees, they like to get into soft drink cans. They land on people's plates and proceed to take a piece of sausage or steak or drink up a little bit of tomato sauce. Try to shoo them away, and they will buzz up around your face and sometimes sting you. The sting is often more painful than a bee sting, and the wasp can sting a number of times because its sting is not barbed like a bee sting and does not get stuck in the skin.

If wasps are about, it is a good idea to spray the garden table and chairs before you start an outdoor lunch.

Sometimes wasp stings are very serious. Some people become very sensitive to wasp stings, like bee stings. When they are stung they must see a doctor at once.

FIRST AID

For wasp stings—
See pages 11–13.

19 Jumper and Bull Ants

There are probably more than 20,000 of these pesky creatures in the bush for every human in Australia. Ever alert, they wait for the picnicker to arrive in the region of their nest. As you will see from the picture, they have a fine pair of nippers at the front end. These are used to grab hold of the victim. The ant then curls its body up and a long fine sting comes out of its behind and is driven into the target. The poison it injects burns and hurts you.

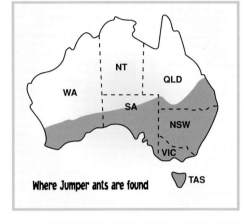

Where Jumper ants are found

If undisturbed, the ant will usually sting a number of times. At a picnic, everyone soon knows that someone has been stung. They usually do a little bit of a dance, and often swear. If the ant has walked up inside someone's jeans, the victim disappears into the bush at high speed.

Where Bull ants are found

Unfortunately, many people have become very sensitive to ant poison, especially to Jumper ant poison. A single sting can make these people collapse and can even kill them. Scientists at the Australian Venom Research Unit are trying to find a safe treatment for them. In the meantime, everyone has to take great care to avoid contact with Jumper ants.

Ants such as these are only found in Australia. They are a very old type of ant, and were busily using their venom to defend their nests millions of years before humans appeared on earth.

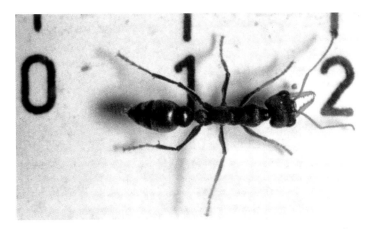

Jumper ant

Bull ant

FIRST AID

For ant stings—
See pages 11–13.

20 The Blue Ant

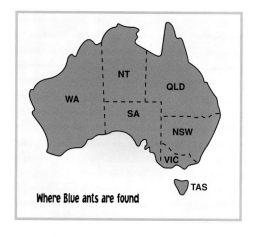

Where Blue ants are found

In fact, the Blue ant is not really an ant at all. It is the name of a wingless female wasp! Blue ants have a very large sting that causes pain straight away and which may last for hours. Their magnificent metallic blue bodies are nearly 3 cm long and certainly attract attention when they are dug up

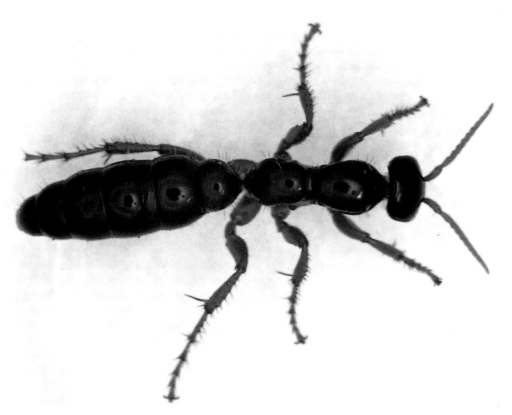

The female Blue ant

by gardeners. If they are picked up, they almost always respond by giving a painful sting. The male, which has wings, is very small and dark, is rarely seen, and has no sting.

The female finds her sting very useful. She digs a tunnel at least 50 cm below the surface of the ground and then hunts down a large mole cricket nymph. After paralysing the nymph with her venomous sting, she drags it to the bottom of her tunnel and then uses her sting to deposit her eggs in the nymph, so that when the eggs hatch they have a nice fresh cricket nymph available for their first feed.

After going to all this trouble one can understand the wasp's anger when a gardener's spade disturbs her important activities.

FIRST AID

For Blue Ant stings—
The same as for Bee stings—
See pages 11–13

21 Scorpions

Where Scorpions are found

Australian Scorpions are not as dangerous as those found in places like the Middle East and Mexico, and you are not likely to get seriously ill after being stung by one of our Scorpions. The further north you go, however, the bigger the Scorpions are, and the greater the amount of poison they can inject.

Scorpions grab their prey with their big front claws and then drive home their sting, which is on the tip of their tails. In humans, the poison produces a very sharp pain that can last for some hours, but in the southern parts of Australia most Scorpion stings are little worse than Bee stings. It is pretty rare to be stung by a Scorpion so people don't become sensitive to their poisons as they do to Ant and Bee stings.

Scorpions are quite cute little creatures and can often be found resting under small rocks in the bush. So keep your eyes open and take care where you put your hands!

FIRST AID

For Scorpion stings—
Apply ice and water for pain relief.

22 The Platypus

Where the Platypus is found

Most people know that the Platypus is a mammal which lays eggs. They know it has a front end that looks like a duck, and that it has a beautiful fur coat that keeps it nice and warm as it swims around hunting for yabbies and worms. What most people don't know is that the male Platypus can give a sting that causes terrible pain.

Inside each rear leg of the male Platypus is a poison spur and when he grips another Platypus (or a fisherman's arm!) with his legs, the spur injects poison. Fishermen have cried because the sting hurts so much.

It is not certain why the Platypus has this poison spur. It may be just to defend itself and its family, or it may have something to do with its mating habits.

It has only recently been discovered that the Platypus can find yabbies and other potential meals under water, in the dark, by detecting the tiny bits of electricity given off by these creatures. Little spots on the Platypus's beak receive this information. Scientists have discovered that the Platypus will find the tiniest battery, even when it is well hidden under rocks. It makes you wonder what other secrets the Platypus has ...

Close-up of spur

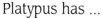

For Platypus stings—
See page 13.

23 Blue-ringed Octopus

Where Blue-ringed Octopuses are found

Like the Red-back spider, this little Octopus has colours that warn you that it is dangerous. Normally it has dull yellow-brown bands with blue circles on its arms and body, but when it is disturbed its colours go dark and the rings become a bright peacock blue.

It has a tiny beak where its 8 arms join, and although it won't bite you in the water, it may if you pick it up. This Octopus is the only very dangerous one in the world and carries enough poison to paralyse 10 adults. Usually it uses this poison to kill crabs so it can eat them without having to fight them first.

People have died after carrying this Octopus on their arms. If you pick it up it will try to escape since it can't breathe when out of the water. It only bites when it is really upset and feels it is about to die. The victim doesn't usually feel the bite, but will very quickly become dizzy and paralysed.

If someone is bitten by this Octopus the first aid is the same as for snake bite and the victim may also need help with breathing.

Never touch these little creatures. If you see them in a rock pool just poke them gently with a stick and watch the beautiful colour changes!

FIRST AID

For Blue-ringed Octopus bites—
- Pressure-immobilisation method—see pages 8-10.
- CPR may be needed—see page 12

WHEN ANGRY,
THE BLUE-RINGED OCTOPUS
SHOWS HIS TRUE COLOURS!

24 Box Jellyfish

In 1956 a new tropical killer was discovered in northern Queensland. Over the years about 60 swimmers had died within minutes of being stung by some animal, but it had never been found. Most stings happened on cloudy, dull days when the sea was calm. A swimmer, usually a child, suddenly gave a terrible

Where Box jellyfish are found

scream, stumbled out of the water and fell over. Victims looked as if they had been struck with whips because their bodies were covered with long red lines. The ones that didn't die had awful scars for the rest of their lives.

This tropical killer turned out to be the Box jellyfish. It is sometimes called the 'Sea Wasp', but this is a bad name as some swimmers have been known to keep looking up into the sky for it in case it is flying about! It is one of the few jellyfish that can kill a person, and when fully grown it has a body the size of a laundry bucket. Ribbons of tentacles stream out from the body and are covered with millions and millions of stinging capsules. The Box jellyfish uses these to sting and kill fish. Then the tentacles pull the dead fish up to its mouth.

FIRST AID

For Box jellyfish stings—
- Pour vinegar (never methylated spirits) over tentacles on the victim's body.
- CPR (see page 12) and antivenom may be needed.
- Seek medical care.

When a swimmer bumps into this jellyfish the thin tentacles get torn off, stick to the victim and inject their poison into the body. Victims should be taken out of water and vinegar (never methylated spirits) poured over the jelly-like tentacles sticking to them. This kills the tentacles so they can be removed without injecting more poison. People who are badly stung may need help with their breathing and the doctor may give them antivenom.

The golden rule is never to swim in tropical waters if the local people say the Box jellyfish may be lurking about. Usually 'jellyfish warnings' are broadcast over radio stations and the lifesavers close the beaches. Don't swim by yourself in the tropics—people may never know what happened to you.

25 The Irukandji

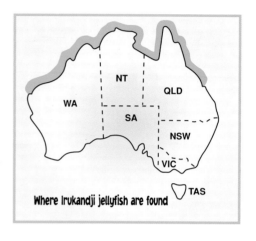

Where Irukandji jellyfish are found

There are three hard things about the Irukandji jellyfish. One is to remember its name, one is to spell it and the third is to see them! The name comes from an Aboriginal tribe that used to live near Cairns. This jellyfish is small: its body is only 2 cm wide and 2.5 cm long. It has four stinging tentacles that may be as long as 65 cm. It is transparent and almost impossible to see in the water. It is easiest to see when it has caught a prawn or small fish. When this happens it looks as if the prawn or fish is moving through the water by itself, but there's something strange about the way it's moving. If it is netted and brought to the surface, the outline of the Irukandji can be seen clutching its dinner!

THIS JELLYFISH IS ALMOST INVISIBLE.

Stings by the Irukandji are more common in summer and may cause a most unusual illness. Usually at the time the swimmer is stung by this jellyfish, the sting does not particularly worry them and they tend to forget about it. However, the absorbed Irukandji venom strikes about thirty minutes later and the

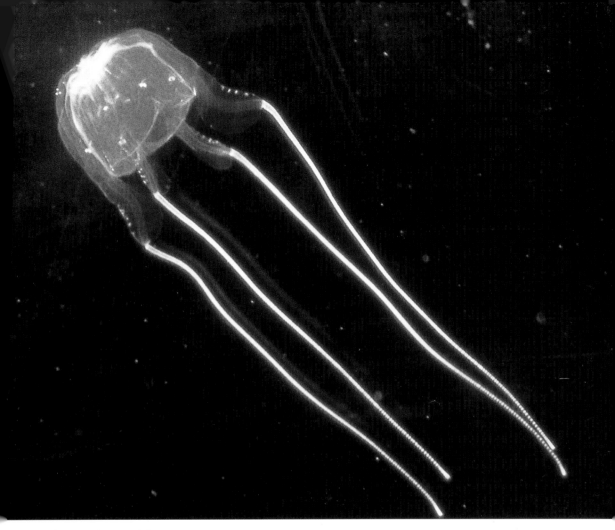

Photo: Bob Hartwick

dreadful 'Irukandji syndrome' starts. This includes severe back and tummy pains which may last for hours, nausea and vomiting, a terrible headache, restlessness, sweating, and very high blood pressure. Doctors have a difficult time treating this disease and so the Australian Venom Research Unit is trying to make an antivenom. Lifesavers use very fine nets to try and capture jellyfish for this research. The problem is, they usually only know where to go out with nets after swimmers have been stung! If only the jellyfish carried flashing red warning lights, life would be easier!

FIRST AID

For Irukandji stings—
As for Box jellyfish stings—see page 60

26 Blue Bottle or Portuguese Man-of-War

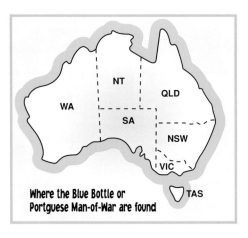

Where the Blue Bottle or Portguese Man-of-War are found

This is a common jellyfish which is found in the warmer seas of the world. The Blue Bottle is actually a number of jellyfish that have all joined together. Its top part has a lot of bubbles that make it light and help it catch the breeze so it sails across the water. Its stinging tentacles float underneath and these may be as long as 10 metres. The arrival of these jellyfish soon closes many beaches around the world.

Swimmers often come in contact with Blue Bottles, which can give quite painful stings, although they are nowhere near as painful as those produced by the Box jellyfish (page 60). Severe stingings have sometimes killed people. The stings often have a ladder-like shape that mirrors the position of the clumps of stinging capsules on each tentacle.

Even bits of the jellyfish that have been broken off can float around and hurt people later on. Swimmers' eyes are sometimes damaged by small pieces of jellyfish.

FIRST AID

For Blue Bottle stings—
See page 13.

Photo: Queensland Surf Rescue

27 Stingrays

Stingrays can grow very big indeed. Some may reach 2 metres wide and over 4 metres in length. The tail itself is quite harmless, but at its base is a sting. Stingrays often lie on the bottom of the sea and if you stand on them, or swim near them, they give a sudden thrust of the tail, which drives the sting into you.

Where Stingrays are found

Their tail works like a trigger, so the sting is driven in with terrible force. It has poison on it, and the wound is extremely painful and often bleeds a great deal. Two Australians died when the sting actually entered their hearts.

Photo: Rudi H. Kuiter

Stingrays are very hard to see when they are resting on the seabed. It is best to go swimming with lots of other people, and being last in the water is probably the safest.

FIRST AID

For Stingray stings— See page 14.

28 Stonefish

Stonefish are a very good reason for not walking about in tropical waters bare-foot. Stand on a Stonefish and it's off to hospital for at least a week. They have 13 very sharp, poisonous spines along their backs.

Where Stonefish are found

Stonefish are the most dangerous stinging fish in the world. When you tread on one, the spines stick up straight and inject their poison deep into your foot. If you put your hand on one, it's the end of your hand for a while. The poison makes your foot or hand terribly painful and swollen and can also affect the muscles of your body.

Even an expert can have trouble spotting a Stonefish as it sits camou-flaged in the shallow waters of coral reefs or mud flats. It may grow to a

BEWARE OF STONEFISH IF YOU PADDLE WITH SOFT LITTLE FEET!

length of 47 cm, is covered with greenish slime and half buries itself in the sand. Its beady little eyes watch for any passing fish which it will suddenly suck in by opening its giant mouth. Some people think it is like an older brother or sister or a politician—it sits around doing nothing all day, it has a big mouth, and can prove highly venomous if you try to shift it!

Although like other fish stings, Stonefish stings can be made less painful by bathing in warm water; usually pain-killing drugs and antivenom from the doctor are needed. Remember, most stings occur during the school holidays—so take care.

FIRST AID

For Stonefish stings—
- Bathe injured area in warm water.
- Seek medical attention—antivenom or painkillers may be needed.

29 Butterfly Cod or Lion Fish

Where Butterfly Cod or Lion Fish are found

This is a beautiful fish that can weigh up to 1 kg and grow as long as 42 cm. Its feather-like fins are soft, but hidden amongst them are eighteen sharp and very venomous spines. When threatened, the fish may point the spines forward a bit like a shield and advance towards you. It tends to be very nosey and will often approach divers. Brushing it aside with a bare hand is not a good idea!

Butterfly cod stings are very painful, and the victim usually has to be helped out of the water. Pain and swelling may last for weeks.

Photo: Keith Gillett

Sometimes Butterfly cod are sold as aquarium fish and the proud owner can be stung accidentally while cleaning the inner wall of the tank. Curious visitors may put a hand in the tank to pat the pretty fish. A few seconds later, everyone in the house, if not the neighbourhood, will know something has happened!

FIRST AID

For Butterfly cod—
See Stonefish and other stinging fish, page 14.

30 Conus Shells

Where dangerous
Conus shells are found

Conus shells are like sea-going garden snails, but they're not quite as harmless to humans. Several types can kill people.

The dangerous Conus shells live in tropical waters. They spend most of their time buried in sand, but move around at night to look for a new base if they've run out of food. They have a special way of catching their food. When a Conus shell sees a nice little fish coming by, it moves its mouth outwards and from there pushes a little poison dart into the fish. The fish is quickly killed by the poison and held close to the Conus shell by the dart. Its mouth then closes over the fish, which is slowly swallowed. About 20 or 30 of these little darts are kept soaking in a pool of poison at the bottom of the shell's mouth. The darts are not used again and more are being made all the time.

Conus shells are often very beautiful and people love collecting them. However, if you pick one up with the owner still alive inside, you could be in dead trouble!

FIRST AID

- Pressure-immobilisation method—see pages 8–10.
- CPR may be needed—see page 12.

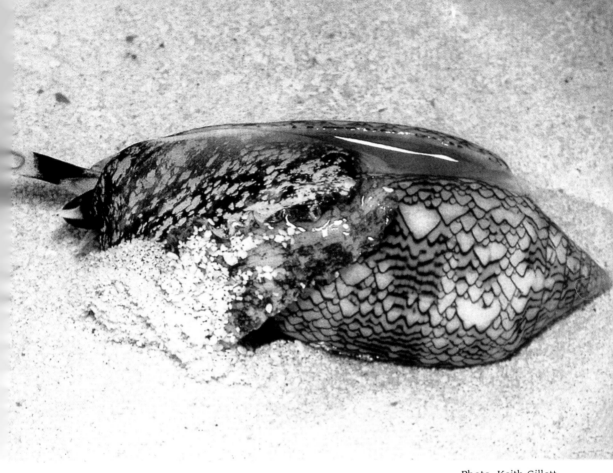

Photo: Keith Gillett

A few years ago, a man held one in his hand on Hayman Island and it fired its little dart into him. He died some hours later from paralysis. Another man put one in his pocket and he got a nasty shock a few minutes later. Many people are stung when they are cleaning the shells as, like some of us, this creature does not like soap and scrubbing brushes.

The shells should not be picked up with bare hands, even at the blunt end, as the animal can almost reach there with its dart. They should only be picked up with thick leather gloves or a pair of tongs.

If someone is stung, the first aid is the same as for snake bite. The victim may need some help with breathing if the sting is bad.

31 Crown of Thorns Starfish

This is a spiky brute. There are only two kinds of venomous starfish known and the biggest and most important is the Crown of Thorns, which is much too common on coral reefs. It feeds on and damages living coral and is causing a huge amount of devastation to the Great Barrier Reef.

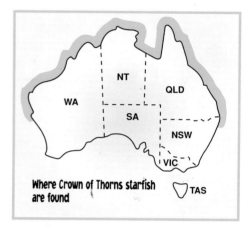

Where Crown of Thorns starfish are found

It is very colourful: its blue arms end with very sharp red-tipped poisonous spines. While most starfish have five arms, the Crown of Thorns can have as many as 23!

It moves over the coral slowly turning its stomach inside out to digest the coral as it travels along. This starfish can breed in huge numbers. The female may produce up to twenty million eggs each year, and if one starfish is cut in half it re-grows into two starfish!

Its extremely sharp spines are tipped with poison, and if they penetrate the skin it can be terribly painful. They should only be picked up with gloved hands. Even when they are found washed up on the beach dead, they may still be dangerous. It's best just to leave them alone.

FIRST AID

For Crown of Thorns—
- Carefully pull out spines, bathe wound in warm, not scalding water. An ice-water pack may also help relieve pain.
- Seek medical advice.

Photo: Kevin Deacon

32 Black Sea Urchin

Creatures don't come much spikier than this one. It has a round, black body covered with needle-sharp, hollow spines. The spines, which may be as long as 30 cm, are used both as its 'legs' and for protection. Each spine is connected to the body by something like a shoulder joint. The Black Sea Urchin usually parks itself during the day and feeds at night on plants and any unmoving (sedentary) animal.

Where Black Sea Urchins are found

If the moving Sea Urchin is disturbed, it immediately rolls itself up into a ball. It is impossible to pick one up from the water using a bare hand without being stung. The spines easily go through the skin, often very deep, before snapping off. They are very painful, and the injured area may become swollen, and possibly black, as pigment spreads out from the spine. The X-rays of a young man who knelt on one showed that the spines went right into his knee joint. Ouch!

SOMEONE IS ABOUT TO DO SOMETHING SILLY!

Photo: Neville Coleman

FIRST AID

For Black Sea Urchin stings—
Carefully pull out any spines, bathe in warm,
but not scalding, water to ease the pain, and
seek medical care.

33 Toad and Puffer Fish

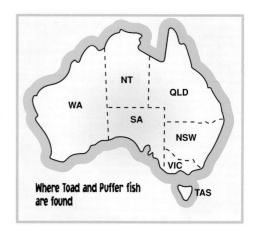

Where Toad and Puffer fish are found

These fish are very poisonous and should never be eaten. The very strong poison is found in the flesh of the fish as well as its insides. It is tasteless and not destroyed by heat, so even cooking them does not make these fish safe.

Puffer and Toad fish are often caught off jetties and piers and come in all shapes and sizes. Most are only about 10 cm long. The biggest one ever caught was 76 cm in length. They have very big eyes, and their sharp, strong teeth are joined together to make four big teeth. No one seems to like them.

When pulled out of the water, they usually puff themselves up with air and become like a ball. Some have spikes that stick out as they swell up. None of these fish have scales, so it is a good idea never to eat fish that have no scales. Even if you are starving, these fish should not be eaten—the poison attacks the nerves and you may stop breathing.

FIRST AID

For Toad and Puffer fish poisonings—
- Make the victim vomit if he or she is fully conscious.
- Seek medical care.
- CPR may be needed—see page 12.

If someone has eaten even a bit of one of these fish and they are fully conscious, they should be made to vomit. (Sometimes tickling the back of their throat helps.) They should also be taken to a doctor.

Incidentally, watch out for Toad and Puffer fish teeth! Sometimes they will nip off the end of a finger or toe!

34 Cane Toad

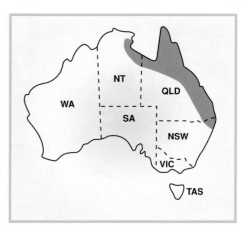

The only good Cane toad is a dead Cane toad. They are big, ugly, and very poisonous. Since they were introduced into Australia in 1935 to eat Cane beetles, they have had nothing but bad PR. When the beetles climbed up the sugar cane so the toads couldn't reach them, the Cane toads turned their attention to breeding. As a result, there are now more than 100 million Cane toads that have descended from the original 101. They breed at a fantastic rate, with the female able to produce 8,000 to 35,000 eggs at one time—and these eggs will hatch within 4 days. Even the eggs are poisonous—although chooks can eat baby Cane toads and survive. Cane toads have spread from Queensland to the Northern Territory and are moving steadily down the coast of New South Wales.

THE CANE TOAD'S POISON KILLS THOUSANDS OF NATIVE ANIMALS AND PETS.

NO-ONE WILL PLAY WITH ME!

Cane toads have large glands on the back of their neck that squirt out poison if they are handled. This poison not only kills vast numbers of Australian wildlife (ranging from native cats to kookaburras, snakes and lizards), but also kills many domestic pets.

Cane toads can grown as long as 23 cm and weigh an impressive 1.25 kg. One Cane toad lived in a

Photo: Bruce Cowell

laboratory for fifteen years, during which time it ate 72,000 cockroaches!

Humans have died after eating Cane toads or drinking soup made from their eggs.

What to do with Cane toads

If you find a Cane toad, the best thing to do is to get an adult to wear gloves and goggles and put it in a plastic bag. The bag should be sealed and lowered into a deep-freeze. A few days later you can bury the toad and re-use the plastic bag to capture the next one.

FIRST AID

After contact with Cane toads—
Wash the exposed area very well with fresh water. If the toxin has been swallowed and the patient is conscious, encourage vomiting and wash the mouth out well with water. Seek medical advice.

Other poisonous animals

Only the most poisonous Australian animals have been described in this book. Apart from the other kinds of poisonous snakes, there are many creatures that can and do make people ill.

On the land, there are other kinds of spiders that give very painful bites.

In the sea, there are dozens of types of stinging fish and jellyfish that can all ruin a holiday.

There are some larger books that describe these land and sea creatures in detail. If you are interested, look for them in your local library. We have listed a few opposite.

Remember, if you take a bit of care you should never be bitten or stung. When you know what the animals look like and keep a safe distance away, neither the animal nor you will be harmed.